the GRADUATE'S HANDBOOK

To _____

From _____

Date _____

the
GRADUATE'S
HANDBOOK

Your No-Nonsense Guide
for What Comes Next

Dr. Clark Gaither

New York

the GRADUATE'S HANDBOOK
Your No-Nonsense Guide *for* What Comes Next

Published in New York, New York, by Morgan James Publishing. Morgan James and The Entrepreneurial Publisher are trademarks of Morgan James, LLC. www.MorganJamesPublishing.com

The Morgan James Speakers Group can bring authors to your live event. For more information or to book an event visit The Morgan James Speakers Group at www.TheMorganJamesSpeakersGroup.com.

ISBN 978-1-63047-923-7 paperback
ISBN 978-1-63047-924-4 eBook
Library of Congress Control Number:
2015921067

Editor:
Shayla Eaton, Curiouser Editing

Cover Design by:
Brittany Bondar

Interior Design by:
Bonnie Bushman
The Whole Caboodle Graphic Design

Shelfie

A **free** eBook edition is available
with the purchase of this print book.

CLEARLY PRINT YOUR NAME ABOVE IN UPPER CASE

Instructions to claim your free eBook edition:
1. Download the Shelfie app for Android or iOS
2. Write your name in **UPPER CASE** above
3. Use the Shelfie app to submit a photo
4. Download your eBook to any device

In an effort to support local communities and raise awareness and funds, Morgan James Publishing donates a percentage of all book sales for the life of each book to Habitat for Humanity Peninsula and Greater Williamsburg

Get involved today, visit
www.MorganJamesBuilds.com

Habitat
for Humanity®
Peninsula and
Greater Williamsburg
Building Partner

To my sister Elaine.

TABLE OF CONTENTS

Whatsoever you write down in this book will come true—with intention. It's all up to you! If you don't write it down, it isn't likely to happen.

Today's date: _____

My 1-Year Goals Are:

_____

_____

_____

_____

_____

My 3-Year Goals Are:

_____

_____

_____

_____

_____

My 5-Year Goals Are:

_____

_____

_____

_____

_____

My 10-Year Goals Are:

_____

_____

_____

_____

_____

My 15-Year Goals Are:

_____

_____

_____

_____

_____

My 25-Year Goals Are:

_____

_____

_____

_____

_____

"Set all of the goals you want. Make all of the plans you want. Provide for contingencies, put backup plans in place, and continually monitor your progress. Still, nothing will prepare you for the ecstasy of success."

— Clark Gaither

"Nothing ever becomes real till it is experienced."
— **John Keats**

"If you are going to search for treasure, let your search begin within. Just know it can be scary. But vast riches await, even in all the darkest places."

— Clark Gaither

INTRODUCTION

The Graduate's Handbook contains a collection of the hardest easy lessons I've ever learned.

I think you should know, though, I was once voted most likely *not* to succeed at anything. At one time, I was an extremely poor student, hung wallpaper and sold stereos for a living, was terrified of public speaking, became an active alcoholic, was a chronic procrastinator, never wrote anything worth reading, and felt like a complete failure.

Yet, for me, it was only because of my mistakes and struggles that I was able to achieve success while learning some valuable lessons along the way. Many of my struggles could have been avoided if I had only listened to those who knew better—but that was not the path I chose.

I want it to be different for you as you begin your journey in this new season of your life.

I want you to begin your journey with a head start and a map with some clear, easy-to-understand directions. I want to give you some no-nonsense advice about what to expect, dispel some common myths, and provide you with unconventional wisdom from some uncommon people.

I wrote this book for you to give you a head start, to maximize your potential for lifelong success. I want you to be the beneficiary of the hardest easy lessons I've ever learned. They are all here within the pages of this book.

Learn. Grow. Share.

— Dr. Clark Gaither

SUCCESS

Before you can have success, you must first define what success means to you. Is it money, a house, a new car, a great relationship, power, fame, a book, or some combination of these? Each may require a different plan, a different strategy. You must be crystal clear on what you want in order to give yourself the best chance of obtaining it.

Success does not follow or favor chance.

It is not enough just to dream. Sure, dreaming is easier than doing. But your dreams are not reality until you make them your reality.

Hoping for success is not a strategy. Only gamblers hope for success. They lose the majority of the time. Las Vegas was built with the money lost by losers. Las Vegas is owned by planners and doers.

We can transform our lives and achieve success with continual positive actions. The image of your preferred future is your call to action. It will take a plan, intentional hard work, passion, and perseverance to make it happen.

Along the way you will succeed some, fail a lot, doubt yourself, be tempted to give up, be excited one minute, and full of dread the next. I know of no other easier, softer way. Just trust your image of your preferred future and ***start***.

"There are many ways of going forward, but only one way of standing still."

— Franklin D. Roosevelt

"You can't get anywhere from where you are standing. You can get everywhere from where you are going."

— Clark Gaither

"It's like driving a car at night. You never see further than your headlights, but you can make the whole trip that way."

— E. L. Doctorow

"Not until we are completely lost or turned around do we begin to find ourselves."

— Henry David Thoreau

"All journeys have secret destinations of which the traveler is unaware."

— Martin Buber

YOUR LIFE'S JOURNEY

You are on a journey—a different journey from everyone else, one of your own choosing. If you like the journey you are on, then you should stay on it if you can. If you are on a journey you do not like, then you should change your bearing and strike out in a new direction. Either way, it is your choice.

Some people say that it isn't the destination; it's the journey. Others say it isn't the journey; it's the destination. It is both. You can't have one without the other.

We are all on a journey toward an uncertain future and unknown destination. Uncertainty brings doubt and fear. The principle of initial position applies. Where and how you end up is determined in large measure by how you begin, determined by the conditions under which you start.

Plan well, begin well, and you will probably end up in a much better place and position than if you had started poorly without a plan.

Your life will also be like a long journey to an unknown destination. Starting out, you will never know precisely where you might end up, when you will arrive, or the routes you will take to get you there. Knowing who you are will guide you on your journey and make your direction more clear and focused.

The word *journey* infers exploration, excitement, the unknown, risk, discovery, and adventure. New journeys, if not foisted upon us, should be actively and aggressively sought. What greater tragedy than to be assigned a single journey in this life?

"I was never so lost as when I stopped searching."
— Clark Gaither

"Let your mind start a journey through a strange new world. Leave all thoughts of the world you knew before. Let your soul take you where you long to be. Close your eyes, let your spirit start to soar, and you'll live as you've never lived before."

—Erich Fromm

"Be fierce in your resolve to choose your own destiny."
— Clark Gaither

"Strength does not come from physical capacity. It comes from an indomitable will."
— **Mahatma Gandhi**

"The purpose of life is a life of purpose."
— **Robert Byrne**

"Be on purpose."
— Clark Gaither

"I would rather die of passion than of boredom."
— **Vincent van Gogh**

"Clarity amplifies passion.
Focus magnifies purpose."
— Clark Gaither

Passion + Purpose = Fully Alive

PURPOSE AND PASSION

Someone may work and say, "Look at what I can do." Someone else may work and say, "Look what I have to do." Someone who has found his or her purpose in life and pursues it with passion will smile while shouting, "Look at what I get to do!"

You watch them work and you begin to wonder if they are working or playing or both. You can tell they *love* what they do. Passion is all over them. It is their persona. They are eager to learn and share what they know as they grow.

You see this almost universally among entrepreneurs who have found joy in their purpose for living. Optimism is rooted in their abundance mentality, where there is no lack in life. For them, there is no end—only the desire to *begin*.

"Energy and persistence conquer all things."
— **Benjamin Franklin**

"My dear friend, clear your mind of can't."
— **Samuel Johnson**

"Try not to die from a really bad case of can't. Trust me, I'm a doctor."
— Clark Gaither

"Given a choice, I would much rather explore possibilities rather than shy away from uncertainties."
— Clark Gaither

"When nothing is sure, everything is possible."
— **Margaret Atwood**

"All progress takes place outside the comfort zone."
— **Michael John Bobak**

LIFE WITHOUT
SELF-IMPOSED LIMITS

"I can't."
"That's impossible."
"I don't know how."

These are powerful words. They hold people back of their own volition. They are dream-stoppers and hope-enders. The mere utterance of these words destroys initiative, stifles creativity, and limits growth. They do not even have to be spoken in order for their full force to be felt. Just thinking these words is enough. How powerful is that?

The phrases "I can't" or "That's impossible" form finite statements. What would be, could be, should be begins and ends with those words. After those words, there is nothing left to add. They are declarations of cessation, of complete arrest, and of conclusion. They are a barricade to further effort. The end.

No one will ever be able to transform his or her life into his or her own preferred future with an attitude of "I can't" or "I won't." Saying "I won't" is a non-starter, a compass without direction, a road without a beginning, a song without music, a book with no words, a canvas without paint.

Saying "I can" means "I am able" to do something. This increases the potential that you *will* do something. Saying "I can" and taking action means no matter what the outcome, you have already won a different future for yourself.

The brain is an amazing organ. What it is unable to do, it can imagine doing. What is imagined creates possibilities. Possibilities have a habit of turning into reality with time and effort. Which makes me wonder: what exactly cannot be accomplished?

Those who have plans for brightening their own futures while brightening the futures of those around them harbor no thoughts of the impossible. Thoughts of the impossible are supplanted by "I have an idea"; "Just imagine . . . "; and "What if . . ."

"If you can imagine it, you can achieve it. If you can dream it, you can become it."

— William Arthur Ward

"What the mind of man can conceive and believe, it can achieve."

— Napoleon Hill

"You are now, and you do become, what you think about."

— Earl Nightingale

"You are the average of the five people you spend the most time with."

— Jim Rohn

"Wouldn't you rather be the architect of your own destiny rather than living your life according to someone else's blueprint?"

— Clark Gaither

"There is only one success: to be able to spend your life in your own way."

— Christopher Morley

People who dare to dream and take the initiative to act on their dreams are possibility-thinkers. They impose no limitations on themselves. You know who they are. You buy their goods and services every day.

"Life has no limitations, except the ones you make."

—Les Brown

"We don't see things the way they are. We see things the way we are."

— Anais Nin

"The question isn't what *do you see* today. It's how do you see today?"

— Clark Gaither

"There is nothing wrong with magical thinking as long as your expectations are vanishingly, ridiculously, infinitesimally small. Magical thinking never produces tangible results."

— Clark Gaither

"You cannot have a positive life and a negative mind."

— Joyce Meyer

"He who knows himself is enlightened."

— Lao Tzu

SUGGESTIONS FOR REALITY-BASED LIVING

There is no such thing as luck. It is an illusion. It is magical thinking. Sustained, persistent hard work with passion and purpose will lead to success. To an independent observer, it just looks like luck.

There is no magic formula, magic wand, or magic fairy dust. There are tried-and-true formulas for success that are not magical and are available to anyone. That is, they will work if you work them. Magical thinking gets you squat.

Serving the needs, wants, and desires of others will bring you *your* needs, wants, and desires. They will come to you from those you serve.

If you are full of discontentment, unhappiness, and discomfiture and are looking for a sign for when to transform your life, your sign is discontentment, unhappiness, and discomfiture.

Your preferred future is your dream and no one else's. Translating your life from where you are to your preferred future is *your* job. No one else will do this for you, because they are concerned about their own lives and preferred futures— not yours.

If you say, "I can't," I will not believe you, even though you will be right 100 percent of the time. My not believing it to be true will make no difference, though, until you stop believing it is true. At which point you will again be right 100 percent of the time. It is the only instance in your life when you will be 100 percent right either way. Your choice.

For anyone insisting on employing the *"I can't"* mentality, let's just get it right from the outset and translate this to what it actually means: *"I won't."* That might sound harsh, but it's the truth.

Praying for God to do something for you that you can do for yourself, to figure out something you can figure out for yourself, or to give you something you can get for yourself is a waste of mental energy, your natural talents, and abilities. Not to mention the good Lord's time. Get to work with what you have, what you have been given, and be grateful. Then God will smile.

The road to success passes through the gateposts of failure every time! There is just no easier, softer way. When you come to a point when you can name failure as a cherished friend, you will have both feet firmly planted pointing toward, or actually within, your preferred future.

We are glorious creatures of the universe destined to accomplish, to build, to produce, to create, to innovate.

You don't hope for good health. You must work at it with an actionable plan and routine maintenance. You will either make yourself healthy with effort or unhealthy through neglect.

Make no mistake: if your preferred future includes drugs or alcohol addiction, you will never have a future. If you already reside in your preferred future and are actively addicted, you will never keep it. All addictions end. Either the addict gets sober or the addict dies of the disease. Of course, every active addict lives in a place where they are going to be different. It is a place called *denial*.

"We say we know others well. Yet we spend much of our life knowing little about ourselves. One of these statements is absolutely true. The other is a gross overestimate."
— Clark Gaither

SELF-INTEREST VERSUS SELFISHNESS

There is a fundamental difference between self-interest and selfishness. Self-interest is a rational, valid concern for one's own well-being. Trying to better one's self while helping others is not only noble, I believe it is our responsibility. If you can make a living while doing it, then so much the better.

Self-interest is healthy. It keeps us learning, creating, growing, and moving forward. It is our responsibility to foster enough self-interest to identify and build upon our own unique set of natural talents and abilities.

Selfish people, on the other hand, are exclusively and excessively concerned with themselves to the exclusion of nearly all else. The selfish person will want what you have without doing anything to get it, other than to ask or demand it for themselves. The selfish constantly seek to pleasure, advantage, or enrich themselves with a complete disregard for others and often at the expense of others.

"There is no self-interest completely unrelated to others' interests. Due to the fundamental interconnectedness which lies at the heart of reality, your interest is also my interest. From this it becomes clear that "my" interest and "your" interest are intimately connected. In a deep sense, they converge."

—Dalai Lama

"Shakespeare once said, 'To be or not to be? That is the question.' Okay. Next question. How do you be happy?"
—Clark Gaither

"If you want to be happy, be."
— Leo Tolstoy

HAPPINESS

The desire for and the power of happiness is universal. Everyone wants to be happy. Not everyone will put in the effort to make themselves happy. Happiness, like everything else in life, is a choice. If you are happy and can passionately share what makes you happy, you will help others choose happiness too.

I have a general sense of what it might take to make happiness easier to obtain for most people who aren't happy.

Embrace, cling to, and devour the positive aspects of living. Read poetry, uplifting books, and inspirational stories. Improve yourself. Learn! Watch comedies. Laugh! Laugh some more. Laugh at yourself.

Avoid negativity. Avoid negativity as if it were a toxin because it will poison the wellspring of your soul. Negativity is anathema to positive change. No one would begin a race while tethered to the ground. Negative attitudes, beliefs, outlooks, forecasting, viewpoints, approaches, and positions are just binders that keep us stuck, running in place. Whether negativity comes from within or from outside ourselves makes no difference.

"Happiness is a how; not a what. A talent, not an object."
—Hermann Hesse

"Most folks are as happy as they make up their minds to be."
—Abraham Lincoln

"Wisdom begins in wonder."

— Socrates

WONDER AND CURIOSITY

N*ever* lose your childlike sense of wonder. If you have lost it, go out and get it back as quickly as possible. I might suggest skipping, a tickle fight, coloring, or making mud pies. If you think I am kidding, I am not.

Adults need to play just like children. Your inner child has never left you. You need it too. The child in you likes to ask questions. Ask away. Ask more questions than you are called upon to answer. That is how we learn. That is how we figure things out.

If you have an abiding curiosity and sense of wonder about you, then there is no end to what you can learn or accomplish. What is now possible for nearly anyone seemed impossible for nearly everyone just fifty years ago. Wonder and curiosity can set people on fire with a fever to innovate.

"Learning never exhausts the mind."
— Leonardo da Vinci

"We are never fully prepared for what we discover."
— Clark Gaither

KNOWLEDGE

Gain as much knowledge as you can before you assume room temperature.

Never stop learning.

If you are going to write, speak, produce, sell, or serve, you will only be successful in doing so from a position of authority. Knowledge will give you authority. Some say experience alone is sufficient, but what is experience other than practical knowledge?

I am not necessarily talking about university degrees here. The entire world's panoply of knowledge is the Internet, our twenty-first-century codex. All knowledge is available to all people, all of the time, everywhere. There is more information out there than you could consume in a thousand lifetimes—most of it free.

Don't know something but need to? Go out, find the necessary knowledge, and learn it. Never stop learning.

> *"There are known knowns; there are things we know that we know. We also know there are known unknowns; that is to say, we know there are some things we do not know. But there are also unknown unknowns—the ones we don't know we don't know."*
>
> **— Donald Rumsfeld**

Don't get stuck by an unknown. Being stuck, paralyzed, or otherwise affected by an unknown, something that could be known, is a choice. Choose to *know* instead.

"The important thing is not to stop questioning. Curiosity has its own reason for existing. One cannot help but be in awe when he contemplates the mysteries of eternity, of life, of the marvelous structure of reality. It is enough if one tries merely to comprehend a little of this mystery every day. Never lose a holy curiosity."

—Albert Einstein

"Nothing that you do will ever feel good if you let people convince you that you have no choice."

— **Fiona Apple**

"Make your first choice the company you keep."

— Clark Gaither

CHOICE

L ife is a series of choices. We choose well, we are rewarded. If we choose poorly, are we also not rewarded by the experience? Do we not gain knowledge and insight? Is our mental metal not tempered? Are we not propelled forward to try again and do better the next time? Isn't adversity our friend?

Consider this then. If you choose well, you are rewarded. If you choose poorly, you lose. But if you choose to learn from failure and grow and come back stronger than before, then looking back, which was the better path for you to take?

"There is no such thing as a real dream. Dreams remain dreams until made real. Without a plan and action, dreams are so much smoke in a mist."

— Clark Gaither

"Help others achieve their dreams and you will achieve yours."

— **Les Brown**

"I believe at many times in our lives we dream of creating, producing, or building something that will satisfy a deep and abiding urge to create. I believe we have a need to have an impact, to leave our mark upon the world. We desire to innovate. Our dreams only seem lofty because there are no ready-made blueprints or guidelines for what we want to accomplish."

— Clark Gaither

"Twenty years from now, you will be more disappointed by the things you didn't do than by the ones you did do, so throw off the bowlines, sail away from safe harbor, catch the trade winds in your sails. Explore. Dream. Discover."

— **Mark Twain**

DREAMS

Most people will give up on their dreams because of fear— the fear that they will fail to realize their dreams. I don't see it as being any more complicated than that. Dreaming is a lot easier to do than taking the risks and doing the work required while attempting to fulfill them.

I feel that an individual's dreams, either consciously or unconsciously, will fit within their abilities to accomplish what is possible for them, whether they accomplish them or not. But a dream is just an endpoint. It is a signpost for a direction only.

Dreaming is only a beginning. I submit that it is the journey that defines the depth and breadth of the dream, the boundaries of which are limited only by the dreamer.

All the truly interesting work, products, art, writing, science, talent, psychology, philosophy, and songs will occur along the journey toward that end, toward the dream.

Unfulfilled dreams are a tragedy and a waste of the power of dreaming. I can't think of a worse scenario than to be at the end of one's life without ever attempting to fulfill one's dreams.

Will we achieve all of our dreams? Of course not. But you are not so wise that you can predict which of your dreams you will achieve and which you will not. I would rather you dream, try, and fail than to have never dreamed at all. Worse still would be to dream and never try. Given a choice, which would you choose?

None of us possess a crystal ball to tell us exactly how our futures will unfold. But I predict that if we are diligent today, if we serve with passion and purpose, if we plant an abundance of seeds using our natural talents and abilities, a bountiful harvest of plenty will follow.

Your harvest will look a lot like your dreams which have come true.

"Your imagination can make you infinite."
— Clark Gaither

"The greatest achievement was at first and for a time a dream. The oak sleeps in the acorn, the bird waits in the egg, and in the highest vision of the soul a waking angel stirs. Dreams are the seedlings of realities."
—James Allen

"Don't be pushed by your problems. Be led by your dreams."
—Ralph Waldo Emerson

"I struck out in search of an epiphany and then I realized, I had just had one."

— Clark Gaither

HOPE

I've been there, hoping for a future that never happened. Oh, I had plans, great plans, plans a plenty. I would think about them and build on them with more plans. I would think how great it would be when all my plans were realized and I hoped they would all come true.

I hoped and hoped and hoped. But nothing ever happened the way I planned. At least not while I was busy hoping.

Hope is not a plan. Hope is not an action. Hope is an idea, cerebral constructs without form or substance.

There are reasons that hope may be preferred to taking action.

Hoping is easy and requires less energy than it takes to work toward a goal or work a particular problem for a solution. Doing requires much more energy and can be hard.

Hoping is 100 percent achievable. Anyone can do it and at any time. Taking action risks failure.

To hope is to procrastinate, which is easy to do. Almost every hope is for something to happen at a later time. Taking action *a priori* means starting now.

Hoping is spontaneous given current circumstances. Taking action may require preparation.

Hoping is instantaneous. Taking action requires time.

Hoping is dreaming and sometimes involves magical thinking. Taking action can only be accomplished in reality.

People hope against fear. Taking action is a purpose for change in spite of fear.

Taking action eliminates the need for hope. Only action can convert a hope into reality. Try not to keep on hoping until you come to room temperature. Do something!

"If you knew that hope and despair were paths to the same destination, which would you choose?"

—Robert Breault

"You have a dream. Get on it. Make it real."
— Clark Gaither

"If you want to truly understand something, try to change it."
— Kurt Lewin

"Change scares the living daylights out of me. Not the possibility of living with change, but of trying to get along without it."
— Clark Gaither

"I changed nothing, and nothing changed."
— Clark Gaither

"Your life doesn't get better by chance; it gets better by change."
— John Rohn

"Embrace change every chance you get."
— Clark Gaither

"I think the most productive thing to do during times of change is to be your best self, not the best version of someone else."
— Seth Godin

CHANGE

Don't fear it, dread it, hate it, or rail against it. Embrace change. Come to know and appreciate the magnificent splendor of change.

> *"If you do not change direction, you may end up where you are heading."*
> — **Lao Tzu**

You are not just representing who you are at any given moment in time, but rather an amalgam too of whom you think you are and who you want to become. It is the summed difference of these that becomes who you are.

How do you get to where you want to be? You get there first in your heart, then in your head, and arrive at last with your feet. Each individual decides. For so many years I changed nothing, and nothing changed. Nothing in your life will change unless you change your life.

People starving for change will often serve fear before they ever serve themselves.

Change is inevitable. Since it is inevitable, I believe it is better to try to choose our changes rather than having change choose us. It is a matter of planning and being proactive and intentional in your actions.

It is always nice to have options or choices. They are branch points on the decision tree of life that allow us to exercise some measure of control over our destiny. Sometimes options are numerous, and we can pick our direction leisurely without a lot of associated anxiety.

Sometimes, our options are severely limited and we are forced to make hard choices. We have all been in the undesirable position of having to choose the lesser of two evils. But wasn't it a series of choices that put us there in the first place?

Ideally, it would be best to have more and better options most of the time and fewer instances where options are wholly constrained in scope with only frighteningly dreadful choices remaining. We can choose to act and be different every day.

"You must be the change you wish to see in the world."
— **Mahatma Gandhi**

Change is everywhere. Isaac Asimov once said, "The only constant is change." Sometimes change is welcome. Sometimes it isn't. No one has a perfect life. Change is often out of our hands, out of our control. It is how we react that determines how we will be affected by change going forward.

Rapid dramatic change is often easier to deal with than slow change over time. Rapid change forces us to react quickly. With slow change, we can become complacent or comfortable, even when the change is undesirable.

We allow ourselves to be fooled into thinking that this is just the way things are for us. We stop growing. We stagnate. We become stuck in variations of sameness. It is better to trade variations in sameness for the permanence of change.

Change doesn't have to be something that just happens to us. It can be a force you can apply on your own behalf. When deciding on change, it is important to explore and be open to all options.

You will arrive at your preferred future only with clarity and focus based on the choices you make.

"Your future isn't something which just happens to you. It gets decided everyday with every decision you make."
— Clark Gaither

"The difficulty, the ordeal, is to start."

— **Zane Grey**

PROCRASTINATION

One thing is certain, if we voluntarily delay an intended course of action despite expecting to be worse off for the delay, then that meets the currently accepted definition of procrastination. This type of forestalling can impair you, in that it is counterproductive, needless delaying.

Procrastination may be due to or a coping mechanism for:

- **Anxiety.** "I'm too anxious over starting or completing tasks, especially new or difficult ones." (This is a form of fear.)
- **Impulsiveness.** "I don't have time for this right now."
- **Perfectionism.** "I can't do it well enough for my standards, so I'm not even going to start."

- **Low self-esteem.** "I'm not good enough to complete the task."
- **Depression.** "I don't have the mental or emotional energy to start or complete my work. This needs attention from a mental or other healthcare professional."
- **Good judgment.** "I have assessed all that I have to do and I am going to put this task(s) off for now because it is less important."

All but the last one of these can lead to decreased productivity and inability to progress. The consequences of procrastination may include:

- **Stress.** Pressure to perform mounts as deadlines approach. In the end, procrastination creates more stress than it alleviates.
- **Guilt.** From avoiding what must be done.
- **Crisis.** Too little time remains to adequately complete the task(s) at hand.
- **Stigma.** The chronic procrastinator becomes know as unreliable.

Try these seven steps to help you stop procrastinating:

- **Remember who you are.** Knowing yourself and what you are likely to do when faced with a new project or task is insightful. Vigilance against old behaviors can serve to usher in needed change.

- **Establish a routine.** Generate a schedule, road map, outline, or strategy for handling a new task and try to stick to it. Practice will make it work.

- **Be realistic.** Know the limits to what you can do. Don't try to complete everything at once. Set attainable goals. Don't overpromise and under deliver. Do just the opposite.

- **Scale down tasks.** Break up large projects into more manageable portions or segments. Work through them one at a time. Avoid jumping around from piece to piece. Forget multitasking. There is no such thing. It is a myth.

- **Ask for help.** Good grief, nobody knows everything about everything and none of us is superhuman. If you get stumped or if there is too much for one person to handle, ask for help. It is not a sign of weakness or ineptitude. It means you're human. All humans need help from time to time. If you uncover a weakness, work on it. That is how we grow, and how we grow is how we gain knowledge. You can also set a weakness aside if it is unnecessary to accomplish your goals. The time may be better spent working on your strengths instead.

- **Deadline with a cushion.** Build a pre-deadline cushion into your schedule that will offer some leeway for the unexpected. This margin of safety is not to be used up because of stalling. The actual deadline is the hard limit for project completion. A self-imposed pre-deadline cushion is set before the actual deadline and affords some usable margin if needed due to circumstances outside of your control.

- **Auto reward.** When the task is completed or the project is shipped on time, take time to rest, reflect, and reset for the next project. Oh, and have some fun. If you have worked this list to your advantage, then you've earned it.

These seven steps can also apply to the other realms of your life. People procrastinate all of the time on beginning a regular program of exercise. Physical, mental, emotional, and spiritual vitality depend on balanced efforts within each.

Procrastination can be a major negative force in your life if you choose to let it exert power over you. It is a roadblock for so many. You are the only one who can place it in front of you and you are the only one who can remove it.

"Procrastination always gives you something to look forward to."

—Joan Konner

"Nothing says work efficiency like panic mode."

—Don Roff

"I think of myself as something of a connoisseur of procrastination, creative a dogged in my approach to not getting things done."

—Susan Orlean

"To start without finishing is just like not starting at all."
— Clark Gaither

"To finish first, you must first finish."
— **Rick Mears**

I'M TOO TIRED

Too tired? Really? The majority of the time, the true meaning of these words is: "I am just too lazy to do that right now" (sloth), "I really don't want to do that" (whining), or "I would rather do that later" (procrastination).

If you are feeling too tired to do something you feel you should be doing, ask yourself this question, "If Bill Gates promised you a million dollars, tax-free, to shovel a dump truck full of gravel *right now*, would you say yes?" I think we all know the answer to that question. You would yell, "Where's the shovel? Get out of my way!"

This newfound, untapped store of energy should tell you what you were at first really saying to yourself: "I'm not sufficiently motivated to do this thing that needs doing."

Motivation, it would seem, is a choice. A choice subject to bribery, at that, which should bring you to a new and universal substitute for "I'm too tired" — "Give me a shovel and get out of my way!"

Think back to a time when you said, "I'm too tired." If your washing machine sprang a leak, could you have mopped up the floor? If your dog had run out the door, could you chase after it to retrieve him? If your child, sibling, or parent needed you, could you have responded?

Most of the time when we say we are too tired, it is because we are tired in our heads more so than in our bodies. So be it. If you need rest, get some. But when you often hear yourself saying, "I'm too tired," stop and ask yourself if you are really too tired or is it something else?

I DON'T HAVE TIME

One of the best excuses is "I don't have time." Of course you have time, if it is important to you. We all get 168 hours each week, no more and no less. While we cannot have any more hours, we all make time for those things we feel are important.

When you trot this excuse out, what you are really saying is, "This is just not important enough for me to do (low priority) right now." Even if you feel that it is a high priority, if you do not act on it, what you are really saying is you aren't all in.

Looking back to those times in your life when you said "I don't have time," were there items you could have taken off your plate and made time if you felt it were important? Were you making a convenient excuse for inaction?

If something is important, you will rally around the concept or task and give it top-of-the-list positioning. That's what successful people do. The people who buy their stuff or make their stuff for them are the ones who say, "I don't have time."

The truth is, I waste time every day. Most people do.

The better substitute for "I don't have time" might be "I am going to create some margin so I will have time if I feel it is important to me. I know I no longer have the time to waste!"

"Lack of direction, not lack of time, is the problem. We all have twenty-four hour days."

—Zig Ziglar

"Action is eloquence."

— William Shakespeare

"See. Do. Be."

— Clark Gaither

*"Don't wait.
The time will never be just right."*

— Napoleon Hill

WAITING FOR
THE RIGHT TIME

The phrase "waiting for the right time" is seductive in its rationale and extremely efficient at inaction. There is no inertia, no movement in these words. Although they serve as powerful blocks to progress, they are also too easily lifted and laid into place.

Besides, what does the "right time" mean, anyway? Do the things we wish to do come with a checklist that must be completed before we can begin? Or is it just some nebulous construct of a notion we generate in our own heads to temporarily make ourselves feel better for not taking immediate action?

How do we know when the right time becomes available other than another feeling? Is that our supreme and infallible test for the right time—when we feel like it?

"I don't care how you feel. I care about what you want. If you listen to how you feel, when it comes to what you want, you will not get it because you will never feel like it."

— **Mel Robbins**

Or is there a popup sign that eventually appears somewhere in our visual field displaying the word *go*? Does the man behind the curtain shout *begin*? Or do we simply reach a point when we have exhausted all of our excuses?

Worse yet, how many times do humans just forget about their high hopes, sterling ideals, trailblazing ideas, amazing potentials and possibilities because it never was just the right time?

How much innovation has been lost in waiting for just the right time? How much pain and suffering could have been avoided? How much individual joy and pleasure could have been created and conveyed to others rather than waiting for just the right time?

Let's be honest here. Each of us already knows just the right time to bind with happiness, secure our families, rise up, use our voices, tell our stories, alleviate suffering, heal the sick, comfort the lonely, feed the hungry, eliminate injustice, innovate, create, inspire, teach, learn, grow, and know using our own God-given unique set of natural talents and abilities.

The right time is *now*.

"If you believe struggle produces tangible benefits, even if you should lose, then to struggle and lose or to struggle and win is to win twice . . . To end a struggle before there is a clear loss or win is to lose twice."

> — Clark Gaither

This is the hardest easy lesson to learn:
"All things are difficult before they are easy."

> — **Thomas Fuller**

"When you feel stuck and don't know which way to turn, forward is always the best heading."

> — Clark Gaither

OBSTACLES AND STRUGGLE

Obstacles need not be barriers. Obstacles have their basis in fear. Steal away the power of obstacles by recognizing them for what they are—cerebral insecurities without form or substance. Like ghosts they pop up, or we trot them out, when we step outside our comfort zones. Yet you are the only ones to see them or hear them, and the only person they scare is you.

Struggle is a precious gift. It is solely responsible for every intuitive leap in human history. If I were never to have another struggle for the rest of my life, I would think the universe had abandoned me, perceiving I was no longer worth the effort.

Battles equate to struggles, which we all face. All creatures struggle. Humans achieve their fullest potential though struggle, if we choose.

To end a struggle before there is a clear loss or win is to lose twice. If you believe struggle produces tangible benefits, even if you should lose, then to struggle and lose or to struggle and win is to win twice. Here is a great secret: when we struggle, we only lose if we choose.

Throughout our lives, we are presented with all types of struggles. Some are relatively benign, such as passing a particularly challenging test. Others may be profoundly impact-filled, such as a devastating personal loss. One thing is certain: if you were presented with a great struggle and overcame it, then you were more than likely better off for it in the end.

Sometimes in life we make bad decisions and suffer negative consequences of those decisions. As a result, we struggle. Sometimes, others make destructive and calamitous decisions on our behalf, decisions we have little or no control over, and we struggle desperately as a result.

In each of those instances, if you overcame the difficulty that was presented to you, did your life not take a new and more positive direction? Did you emerge from your struggle forever changed, as in more resolute, stronger, happier, more determined, more content, and better equipped for the next challenge?

If so, what do you think now of your life's greatest struggles? Are they something to disparage or celebrate? Should we despise them or be grateful for them?

Struggle will get the ball rolling for you. Step out of the way of yourself and learn from it.

Imagine a life without struggle. How would we learn? How would we grow? How would we become strong? It only takes a moment's reflection to realize that struggle is a precious gift.

The next time you are presented with a great struggle, resolve to overcome it and dwell on these possibilities instead of the dread.

- This struggle could be a prelude to greatness.
- This struggle could be a signal for eminent growth.
- This struggle could lead me off in exciting new directions.
- This struggle could reveal to me some of life's best-kept secrets.
- This struggle could allow me to discover my true passion and purpose.
- This struggle could bring me unanticipated opportunities for joy and happiness.

We gawk at highly successful individuals, and it seems everything is going their way. It seems they can do no wrong and everything they touch becomes gold. We are seduced into thinking this is always how it has been for them. We tell ourselves they are the lucky ones and we will never have such luck.

What we didn't see was all of the effort that preceded their success, the years of struggle, sacrifice, and failure. Every successful individual has laid a solid foundation for success and placed himself or herself in a position to garner win after win. Even so, those who are successful still have losses, but the odds are definitely in their favor due to their continual, steadfast efforts.

"The world breaks everyone, and afterward, some are strong at the broken places."

— Ernest Hemingway

"With everything that has happened to you, you either feel sorry for yourself or treat what has happened as a gift. Everything is either an opportunity to grow or an obstacle to keep you from growing. You get to choose."

—Wayne Dyer

"If you find a path with no obstacles, it probably doesn't lead anywhere."

—Frank A. Clark

"One day, in retrospect, the years of struggle will strike you as the most beautiful."

—Sigmund Freud

"Strength and growth come only through continuous effort and struggle."

—Napoleon Hill

"When you do what you fear most, then you can do anything."

— Stephen Richards

"Let's put fear to rest, shall we? It has had enough exercise."

— Clark Gaither

"Fear is a darkroom where negatives develop."

— Usman B. Asif

"It isn't about being fearless; it's about bringing the negatives out into the light."

— Clark Gaither

"Everything you have ever wanted is on the other side of fear."

— George Addair

"Sometimes our search must take us places we do not want to go. The dark places we fear the most aren't on the outside; they are deep on the inside."

— Clark Gaither

FEAR

You were more fearless in your youth. Everyone was. You were eager to try the new, the different, the riskier and edgier things. What you lacked in knowledge, resource, and expertise you made up for in overconfidence. Everything seemed possible.

As you age and reach your prime, fear will begin to show up and preside over most of the battles and wars within. You became afraid of losing. We traded ignorant fearlessness for educated over cautiousness. Too much began to look impossible to you.

There are hundreds of thousands of quotes, sayings, proverbs, articles, and books about how to handle fear. I am sorry to say I have no magic words, wand, fairy dust, or elixir for eliminating fear. If there were just one thing out there to eliminate fear that worked for everyone, then there would be just one thing out there. That is the truth. What I can offer is some advice well rooted in experience.

People put off so many things in life, too many things, due to fear. You will be presented with opportunities to be different, to change, to grow, to be challenged, to learn, to build, to produce, to love, to help others in profound ways. Strive to set aside your fears. Fear is what will hold you in place until your end comes, if you allow it.

Of course, life *will* knock you down. Life knocks everyone down, multiple times. The question is, will you stay down or rise up? Will you keep getting up or one day just give up? Will you give in to fear and take up residence on the mat?

You will see people all around you get knocked down. Some of them will keep getting back up time after time. Why?

For those people—the ones who keep getting back up—staying down is not an option. They get back up because they will not consent to stay down—they are not content to give up. In fact, you would never be able to hold those people down. *Be* one of those people.

Now, a little bit of fear can be healthy. It can keep us on our toes, motivated and moving forward, keeping us prepared, watchful, and vigilant to our mutual good advantage. Too much fear can be paralyzing.

Fear is a state of being, not an action. You could be courageous and still be afraid. So what is the state of mind or feeling opposite of fear? It is a state of mind we all seek, whether we can name it or not. It is the place in our mind where all is calm, content, quiet, tranquil, restful, and peaceful. It is called *serenity*.

The emotional power behind the word *fear* can be overwhelming, destabilizing, destructive, paralyzing, painful, and ruinous. Or it can be motivational, self-preserving, transforming, actuating, incentivizing, persuasive, and provocative.

Who gets to choose? I think you should know the answer to this question by now. You do, dear reader, you do.

So much human behavior is dictated by fear. Our center for fear is deeply buried in our primitive brain. We can't escape it, nor would we want to escape it completely. It serves a useful purpose in keeping us from harm. However, left unchecked, fear can be paralyzing. We should allow our fears to watch over us, not rule over us.

Remember: fear is just a mental thought process, a gray matter construct, a cerebral conjuring without fabric or form. Fear can and will bend to your will.

"There are days when rain is preferable to sunshine, whether we feel like it or not. Life's storms will come and go. My best advice: learn to like running in the rain."

— Clark Gaither

FAILURE

The road to success will always lead through the gateposts of failure. We all fear failure. Why?

Failure is one of the first lessons we learn in life. We try to sit up, and we slump over. We try to stand up, and we drop back down onto our butts. We try to walk, and we stumble and fall. We try to speak, and nothing intelligible comes out of our mouth. So it goes.

People fail. People will fail repeatedly throughout their lives. This does not make us failures at living. It is how we learn and grow. Life challenges us so we can be more than a resource-absorbing, waste-producing lump of tissue.

What about success? Are humans born a success? No. Are humans born to be successful? Yes, I believe we are. But success comes at the price of failure. Does anyone get to be a success in life without failure?

The road to success is never straight. There are no signposts pointing the way. There is no route to get there that works for everyone, and the last stop before Successville is Failure City.

Look up the word *failure* in the dictionary and you will see defining words such as *unsuccessful, nonperformance, insufficiency, deterioration, decay, bankrupt, insolvency* with synonyms such as *breakdown, decline, deficiency, wreck,* and *defeat.* It is all so negative.

Really? Is this the terminal result for failure 100 percent of the time? Is this all you get from failure, less or nothing at all?

A less-than-expected or negative result does not automatically mean failure. I submit that it *never* means failure. A negative result is still a result and therefore has positive value or potential. Each time we say we fail at something, we learn something valuable, if we so choose. Our "failures" are a form of forward payment for learning those valuable lessons.

Repeating what is taught is learning what is already known. Where is the risk in that? Where is the mystery in that? Attempting to create something new and failing in the attempt is a voyage of self-discovery, something you won't learn in a classroom.

A classroom is where learning takes place. Life outside the classroom is where your education takes place.

Here is a really important equation you should memorize:

Failures + Success = More Success

"If you can see the magic of being here, of just being alive, you can face the day with renewed confidence that in this big old universe and in the grand scheme of things, you mean something."

— Clark Gaither

If down, look up.

"The world woke to something extraordinary today, something singularly unique.
You."

— Clark Gaither

RESILIENCE

Being able to adapt, cope, adjust, confront, carry on, endure, survive, move on, or move forward—these are all qualities of resilience. Too many people who lack resilience get stuck. They suffer the same tragedy or the same trauma over and over again. They stop growing. They stop enjoying life. They stop trying to better themselves. It doesn't have to be that way.

A lack of resilience can leave people paralyzed to the point of being unable to move forward. Everyone should have this trait because the consequences of a lack of resilience can rob you of a brighter future.

Difficulty, tragedy, hardship, and suffering will come to everyone in one form or another if you live long enough. That is just living life on life's terms. We might not have a choice in the bad stuff that may come our way in life, but we do have a choice in how we respond.

Here are nine ways to build resilience:

- Become more self-aware.
- Hold on to the big picture.
- Let time be your friend.
- Get moving.
- Learn acceptance.
- Set goals and move toward them.
- Be optimistic and avoid negativity.
- Have a strong social network.
- Be kind to yourself.

Resilience and hardiness are learned behaviors. We are not born with these attributes; we acquire them. If we lose them, we can reacquire them. If someone has never acquired them and has poor coping skills, it is more difficult to develop them but not impossible. It only requires effort and a willingness to change.

"That which does not destroy, strengthens."
—Friedrich Nietzsche

"We must let go of the life we have planned, so as to accept the one that is waiting for us."

— **Joseph Campbell**

EXPECTATIONS

Expect more from yourself than everyone else.

Things you think are going to be great—the best things that can happen to you—are more than likely going to turn into a steaming pile of excrement.

Things you think are going to be god-awful—the worst things that could happen to you—will turn out to be simply the best and most memorable events of your life. Time will show you the difference.

THE FOUR REALMS

There are four realms you must look after and nourish if you are to have a happy and successful life. They are the mental, emotional, physical, and spiritual realms.

The sense of well-being that you seek is a balance between all four of these realms. Care for three and ignore any one, and your life will be out of balance.

Maximum mental acuity requires continual learning and positive inputs.

Emotional anguish is worse than physical pain, and for this reason emotional well-being is absolutely required for happiness.

The physical realm is the realm most often ignored. To do so will place you in peril.

If you feel disconnected from the world and everyone in it, your spiritual realm has been damaged or neglected.

YOUR MENTAL REALM

S timulate and nourish your brain. These are one and the same. First, unless you are watching something purely educational, turn off the television. Most of what is on TV is crap and will make you stupid. If you must watch something for mindless entertainment, keep it under an hour a day. But just remember, they don't call it mindless for nothing.

Second, I can't think of anything that will get your idea machine cranking faster than reading great books! Pick your area of interest and read to find out what you don't know. Sometimes, you might not even know what you don't know, or what you need to know, until you start reading.

Also, pick books on topics at the periphery of your interests but are in support of your interests. For instance, you might have a great idea or make a great product, but you are going to have to eventually market that product, so books on marketing are a must.

Read inspirational and uplifting books for at least thirty minutes each day. This is the best way I know to switch your brain to transformative thinking. This is something all successful people do, and I wholeheartedly endorse this too.

Read off-topic books and periodicals as well to stimulate your thinking. Foster a hobby. Read poetry and awesome quotes. Listen to a variety of music and podcasts that interest you.

Go out and find the tools that you will need for your success. You simply can't fix something or create anything without the necessary tools. I can't tell you how many people I talk to who complain of some problem that they are unable to solve—yet when I ask them what research they might have done in order to solve their particular problem, all I get in return is a blank stare or "Nothing" or "I don't know" in reply.

Good grief. We have the world at our fingertips these days with smartphones, computer tablets, and laptops. Virtually any problem you might come up with has already been addressed by someone else whose answer is posted on the Internet. There is more information out there than you could possibly review in a million lifetimes, most of it free.

Don't be your first and last barrier to learning whatever it takes to propel you forward.

YOUR EMOTIONAL REALM

Emotional anguish can be worse than physical pain.
If the state of Happiness is a healthy mind, body, and
spirit, then the capital city would be Emotional Well-Being.

Good emotional health doesn't automatically rain down on
you from the sky as you sit and contemplate all that is wrong
with your life. Emotional balance is something that can and
must be cultivated and developed. Like anything else in life that
is worthwhile, it takes choosing differently for yourself, some
effort, some practice, some patience, and plenty of time.

Psychologists have found that chronically happy people
turn out to be more successful across many life domains than
people who are less happy. Makes sense. The surprise was that

their happiness is in large part a direct consequence of their positive emotions and attitudes rather than from their success.

The people were happy before they were successful. They became more successful because they were happy. Here it is in a nutshell:

$$Happiness = Success$$

Therefore,

Success does not always equal happiness.

Like so much else in life, the attitude you have about anything and everything is a personal choice, a mindset.

YOUR PHYSICAL REALM

You ou will always be in better physical shape in your head than you will be in your body.

If you don't do very much, soon you will be unable to do anything. No matter how much you want to do it.

Your will never be the best you can be, the best you can become, if your physical house isn't in order.

Becoming the person you want to be, living the life you want to live, doing the kind of work you want to do is going to require some effort. Being physically fit will help you to accomplish the work that will be required to reach your goals. It isn't absolutely necessary, but it will make your life a whole lot easier and much more enjoyable.

To be more mentally fit, you must become more physically fit. You might ask, what has one to do with the other? I have never seen a mentally fit patient who felt as mentally or emotionally sharp as they were capable of feeling if they felt poorly in their body.

Similarly, I have never seen a patient who was physically fit feel well in their body if they were suffering emotionally. We all live inside our heads. What we "feel" is a summation of our emotional, mental, spiritual, and physical feelings.

Try to establish a habit of regular cardiovascular exercise.

Here is some tried-and-true sage advice if you don't feel good and are overweight, eat poorly, don't exercise, recline in the La-Z-Boy to watch TV in the evening after dinner, drink too much alcohol or smoke, can't hold out to do anything, and don't feel good: lose weight, eat healthy, stop bad behaviors, exercise regularly until you can hold out to do anything, burn your La-Z-Boy, then your TV, and feel better. It's really not that complicated.

"A yogi never forgets that health must begin with the body....Physical health is not a commodity to be bargained for. Nor can it be swallowed in the form of drugs and pills....It is something we must build up. You have to create within yourself the experience of beauty, liberation, and infinity. This is health."

—B. K. S. Iyengar

"To be filled up on the inside, you must be open to what exists on the outside."

— Clark Gaither

YOUR SPIRITUAL REALM

The spirit encompasses your sense of who you are, why you are here, and your place in the world. It represents your connectedness, or lack of connectedness, to other people, to nature, and to reality. Your spiritual health is reflected in your sense of purpose and in your attitudes toward the world and everything and everyone in it.

How is your spiritual health? Do you feel connected to humanity, a higher power, nature, and the world around you? Do you have a sense of purpose and hope for the future? Do you face each day with excitement and optimism? Do you have a sense of peace, calmness, and serenity? If so, you are in excellent spiritual health.

Or do you live in fear under a prevailing sense of dread, feel you walk alone in this world, prefer pessimism over optimism, feel hopeless or helpless, feel empty or apathetic, or feel anxious for the future? Do you feel you know who you are and have a sense of purpose? Or are you somewhere in between these two extremes? If so, then your spiritual self may be damaged or suffering.

For improved spiritual health, practice mindfulness. If there is something that you really enjoy, then slow down and savor everything worthy of your time and attention. Practice kindness, patience, the art of grace, empathy, and compassion. Be decent and tolerant. Be honest.

Mindfulness will give you the opportunity to choose better for yourself. It will allow you to consider all of your options in accordance with your core values. Then you will be free to choose better for yourself, free from damaging emotions, which if left unchecked will hold sway over you. Mindfulness will allow you to enjoy being fully alive.

Study art. Start with what you like, and then branch out. Take an art class. If you say that you aren't artistic and are of the opinion that artists are born artists, I will tell you that you are wrong. If artists are born, then there are just over seven billion of them on the planet and you are one of them. Take an art class, and prove me wrong.

Listen to uplifting music. Again, start with what you like or are familiar with and branch out from there. If you can make music, then create it and then make some more. Make music with others. Make music for others.

Connect with other people. Become part of a community. Well, except the Nobody Loves Me, Everybody Hates Me Community. That one is off-limits. But look around. There are so many different and interesting communities out there to which you can belong. Pick one that will capture your interest and keep you energized.

Connect with animals. Do you have a pet? Some of my most cherished memories are of my pets. There are powerful words and stories that connect people and their pets. Pets can bring out the best in people. They will teach us valuable lessons, if we let them. Do you have stories about a beloved pet?

Laugh. Laugh again. Laugh some more. Especially at yourself. Go to a comedy club. Watch some of the old comedy routines that made you laugh when you were younger. You can find them all on the Internet.

Give of yourself to others. Give your time. Volunteer. Help those less fortunate. Open your heart. Open your mind. In all things, try to be positive. Avoid negativity like it will kill you because it will if you let it. Share your powerful words with others.

Finally, love yourself. You are not some pitiful, worthless creature to be loathed and despised, deserving of the worst the world has to offer. You are a luminous being, a child of the universe. My God, there is only one of you. Laugh, love, live.

Do not deny yourself the wonders life in this world has to offer.

"Who looks outside, dreams; who looks inside, awakes."
—Carl Jung

"I dwell in possibility."

— Emily Dickinson

YOU ARE AN ARTIST,
OR CAN BE

Art is created when an emotional connection is established between the art and the artist, the art and the observer, or both.

Art, true art, is creating something of personal significance that moves you and others emotionally. The medium for this exchange seems secondary.

Each of us has the ability to create using our unique natural talents and abilities. Each of us has the ability to express how we feel through what we create.

When you create something you will connect with it emotionally. Rest assured, there is someone else out there who will feel that connection too. That is art. As such, we have an obligation to create using our own natural set of talents and abilities.

Your profession doesn't matter. The vehicles or materials you use when creating art don't matter. If you are alive, are engaged, can interact, and can connect with others on an emotional level through what you can create, then you are an artist. For no other reason, people are artists because they choose to be.

Don't worry that not everyone will like your art. Not everyone gets or likes Picasso. Many influential people thought Ernest Hemingway's writing was garbage. You don't want or need everyone to like your art. You want those you connect with on an emotional level to like your art. You know what? They will.

People will take notice and recognize you for what you have shared of yourself because of the emotional connection they will feel when they see it. It will help them in some way, and they will thank you for it. They will call you an artist.

If you are serving others with passion and purpose in any capacity using your own unique set of natural talents and abilities, then you are an artist.

We know some works of art are great because they move us and cause us to pause and be changed by it. We connect with it because some other lonely, happy, sad, frustrated, anxious, imperfect, glorious, offensive, flawed, hopeful human being has splattered their heart and soul onto a canvas, a piece of metal, or between the pages of a book.

We laugh or cry with them and celebrate their art with them because we are compelled to do so by what they have created. The great artists would create great art even if it were placed in the woods and no one were around to see it because they must.

The artist knows they did their best, what they had to do, and that is enough for the artist. Whether they realize it or not, the great artists discovered the key to creating great art requires only one thing: passion for one's purpose for being.

"Live as if you were to die tomorrow.
Learn as if you were to live forever."

— **Mahatma Gandhi**

TIME

Always moving forward, time's arrow points in but one direction. The path before you has many branches, but they are all in front of you. The only choices you have are in what direction forward you will go and what you will do along the way. Revisiting the past for the purpose of changing it is not allowed. It is a universal law.

The following are absolute truths:

We only make time for those things we feel are important.

We manage our own schedules by the choices we make.

When you say yes to one thing, you are saying no to
something else.

The best use of the time you have been given is to do
your best to identify your purpose in life and to pursue it with
passion using the unique set of natural talents and abilities you
have been given. I can think of nothing better to do. Can you?

Einstein was right. How time is perceived and measured
depends on one's frame of reference. Time seems to fly by when
times are great, as if it were compressed. Doesn't it? Conversely,
as we lose ourselves in our troubles, time seems to stand still and
never end, as if it has been dilated or expanded.

Everyone has used the phrase, "I don't have time."
Sometimes we don't. Sometimes we do. It is an easy thing to say
when you just really don't want to do something.

We all prioritize our daily lives. We make time for those
things we feel are important. Everyone has a mental list of
things that need to be done on some timeline. Some are
more important than others. As time goes by, we edit the list,
removing items we feel have become less important and adding
others we feel have now become more important.

You make choices when editing your list of priorities.
Sometimes, we suffer consequences as a result of the choices
we make. Sometimes we like to blame others for the choices we
make by putting them in charge of our list of priorities.

Others take full responsibility for their list and conduct their lives accordingly. They have learned the truth. They accept they are the only one in charge of their list of priorities.

Concerning time, Delmore Schwartz wrote, "Time is the fire in which we burn." If we can stick with this metaphor, which I think is brilliant, then you should strive to burn as brightly as you can without burning out.

You never want to just smolder either.

MONEY

To have more, become a minimalist.

Stay out of debt.

If there is something you want and it is a big-ticket item, but you are going to use it less than every couple of months, like a big boat or a vacation home, don't buy it! Rent it for a day or a week. This works well for many smaller ticket items as well. Remember: whatever you buy, you must also maintain.

Produce more than you consume, and save the difference.

Remember: money is just a tool. There are many tools available other than money that can accomplish any given task.

Money's greatest power doesn't lie in its ability to buy you ubiquitous stuff. Money can provide freedom in many different arenas of your life and with that comes peace of mind. There is nothing more precious than freedom.

If you want to help a lot of people, I suggest you find ways to make a lot of money. Remember, it is much easier to give from a cup which is overflowing with abundance than from a cup which is empty or nearly so. The more money you make, the more people you can help. It is really not that complicated.

If you should become very successful through persistent hard work, resourcefulness, and ingenuity, using your own unique set of God-given talents and abilities, don't ever, ever apologize for your success. If you find people around you criticizing your success, find new people to be around. Find people who will celebrate your success as you celebrate theirs.

"It's not hard to make decisions when you know what your values are."

— Roy E. Disney

DECISIONS, DECISIONS

In the time it takes to blow out a candle, your life can instantly and dramatically change—forever. Every day we all make decisions and then act on them. Sometimes, decisions are made and actions are taken by others on our behalf that directly or indirectly affect us whether we want them to or not, with or without our permission.

Sometimes other people's decisions are welcome, sometimes they aren't. We cannot control the decisions and actions of others; all you can control is how you react to them. Ultimately, it is only your own decisions and actions that you can directly control.

How much you allow the actions of others to affect you is a choice, a personal decision. We have all, at one time or another, assigned to others our own self-generated, painful, negative emotions in response to something we did not like. We effectively put others in charge of our feelings.

We allow our own perceptions and interpretation of what has transpired to harm us. We lay off the responsibility of our own insecurities to others, letting them dictate our feelings of happiness or sadness, success or failure, well-being or disquiet.

It is so easy to do. It is human nature, I suppose. Stopping this bad habit is not easy, but not impossible. Strive for progress, not perfection.

What you can do, very effectively if you choose, is control your own decisions and actions. This can be the case whether you are acting or reacting. This is particularly true when it comes to the choices you make. If mistakes are made in the course of everyday living, saying, "He made me do this" or "she made me do that" is just one great big self-delusion.

In the time it takes to blow out a candle, you can choose how you will react to others. You can choose what you will do today to better yourself and your life. Your decisions are yours to make and no one else's.

"I am not a product of my circumstances. I am a product of my decisions."

—Stephen Covey

"Nothing ever goes away until it has taught us what we need to know."

— Pema Chödrön

"I make the most of all that comes and the least of all that goes."

— Sara Teasdale

"If it is gone, let it go."

— Clark Gaither

REGRET

You will have regrets. I believe everyone has or will have regrets, whether they will admit to them or not. If someone says they have absolutely no regrets, then I believe they are either in denial or they just haven't lived long enough yet.

The word *regret* can forever constrain you or liberate you depending on what kind of power you give it, negative or positive. It is okay to have regrets. What you do with them is another matter. Through context and perspective, we can square what we truly regret with what we gained or learned from the circumstances that caused the regret.

Whether this word has a positive or negative influence in your life is a matter of perspective. What influence it will have on the remainder of your life is a matter of choice.

There is always something to be learned from your mistakes, especially the big ones. If, only if, you let the great teacher, life, guide you. Become a willing student.

"Experience is the best teacher, but the tuition is high."
— **Norwegian Proverb**

"Regret for the things we did can be tempered by time; it is regret for the things we did not do that is inconsolable."
—Sydney J. Harris

"If something is out of reach, there is a natural inclination to stretch in order to reach it. Why not in all things stretch? There must be a reason it feels so good to stretch."

— Clark Gaither

"If you want to achieve greatness, stop asking for permission."

— **Anonymous**

"The days of needing someone else's permission to manufacture or sell products or produce art, music, literary works, or crafts are over! All doors either are (or will) open now. The only step remaining is for you to give yourself permission to begin."

— Clark Gaither

ENTREPRENEURS

Find an entrepreneur, and you will find optimism; that's where the energy comes from. I think we should surround ourselves with entrepreneurs.

Better yet, I think everyone should become an entrepreneur.

If you haven't started this noble quest of continual self-improvement and self-discovery, what are you waiting on? Who are you waiting on?

The only one that needs to show up is you! The quest will provide you with everything else you need.

But you must begin.

WORDS AND THOUGHTS

The power of story lies only in the telling.

No one says **no** louder than the voice in your own head.

You must learn to embrace the urgency of now.

Hope is not a plan.

Emotional energy is conductive.

Although entrepreneurs will have different business plans, a different focus, different goals, or varying amounts of expertise, all seem to share one overriding essential quality: eternal and effervescent optimism.

If being a redneck is a glorious lack of sophistication, as Jeff Foxworthy suggests, then being human is a glorious lack of perfection.

If you want to fundamentally change your thinking, you must *start* by changing your thinking.

As I think about life in general, I believe there are two ways lives are lost. Of course, the ultimate way is by death. The other way a life can be lost, perhaps a more tragic way, is a life that is wasted.

There is so much in this world to experience and our time here is finite. Experience as much as you can as often as you can before you assume room temperature.

Try to do something new and different every day.

Perspective is everything, or nothing.

"Violating your core values will lead to burnout at work, in your personal life and on living."

— Clark Gaither

YOUR CORE VALUES

Everyone has a set of core values that are integral to who you are or even who you profess to be. Your core values may change slightly throughout the different seasons of your life, but they are always with you. When you form an opinion, make decisions or judgments, you are either honoring or dishonoring your core values in the process.

We all make choices. All of us will experience consequences as a result of our choosing. If you choose poorly for yourself, the consequences are likely to be undesirable. Alternatively, choosing based on a true reflection of who you are will help to ensure more positive outcomes.

Knowing your core values will offer crystal-clear insight into who you are. This should then be used as a guide when making both the large and small decisions affecting your life and the lives of those around you.

Decision-making guided by core values help immensely when choosing a career, a particular job, a mate, friends, associations, even a home or a car. Deciding in this way, in favor of your own core values, promotes synergy between yourself and the life you chose to live; and synergy promotes harmony.

No matter what career or vocation you have chosen, when you begin to work and share your life's experiences with others, you should tap into your core values and seek to honor them in any and every way possible.

When you are getting ready to make a decision, large or small, do you consider whether or not the decision or potential outcome is in line with your core values? Have you ever taken an inventory of your core values? Can you name them?

If you have never taken a Core Values Inventory, then I invite you to do so. It is easy, doesn't take much time, and it's free. Go to www.clarkgaither.com.

"Your core values are the deeply held beliefs that authentically describe your soul."

—John C. Maxwell

"I thought deeply about this. I ended up concluding that the worst thing that could possibly happen as we get big and as we get a little more influence in the world is if we change our core values and start letting it slide, I can't do that. I'd rather quit."

—Steve Jobs

"The difference between you yesterday and today is the difference you can make today."
— Clark Gaither

"Act as if what you do makes a difference. It does."
— **William James**

SHARE

Share your success by doing exactly what made you successful in the first place. There are many ways to share your success. Here are a few.

1. Seeing to the needs of others by providing added value to your employer, clients, customers, or followers. Especially by providing value that is unexpected or unanticipated.
2. Give away some of your own products, like your book, resources, and promotional items. If you are going to survive in business today, then you had better learn how to give before you ask.

3. Help others as they struggle to become successful. Helping others helps them and you. Not only is it the right thing to do, but it is a win-win.

4. Leverage your success in order to help worthy causes that have captured your interest and when you do, feel good about it. There is nothing wrong with that.

5. Don't ever stop working, producing, and sharing, as long as you are able. If you do, you will rust or your brain and body will rot. Besides, there isn't anyone else like you on this planet. The world will lose the gift of you if you were to just quit. As long as you draw breath, strive to contribute by designing, building, planning, doing.

I don't believe sharing is social responsibility. I believe it is a personal responsibility. Success breeds success. Helping others to achieve is the pathway to personal growth and further success.

If there is much you wish to share, become successful. Be the best you can be at whatever you do using your own unique natural set of talents and abilities. Make truckloads of money if you are able. The more successful you are able to become, the more you will be able to share. It is easier to share from a cup that is overflowing than from a cup draining dry.

Learn. Share. Grow.

FINAL WORDS
AND THOUGHTS

"Be who you are and say what you feel, because those who mind don't matter, and those who matter don't mind."
— Bernard M. Baruch

"If you do not change direction, you may end up where you are heading."
— Lao Tzu

We have heard it all of our lives. The message has been clear. Don't stand out. Conform. Be like everyone else. Dress like everyone else. Listen to the same music as everyone else.

Eat like everyone else. Look like everyone else. Buy stuff and go into debt just like everyone else. How free are you feeling today?

> *"Freedom lies in being bold."*
> — Robert Frost

Boldly Different + Freedom = Happiness

To get noticed, you must stand out from everyone else.

Different = Noticed

Be different!

Let's say you had a heart condition that required open-heart surgery. What level of commitment would you demand of your heart surgeon?

Let's say for the sake of your own personal growth and happiness, you need to change jobs, end a relationship, or begin a new business. What level of commitment are you willing to offer yourself?

Plan + Execution = Results
Plan + Execution + Commitment = Success